East Indian Delights

East Indian Delights

Authentic Vegetarian Recipes from
Karnataka, India

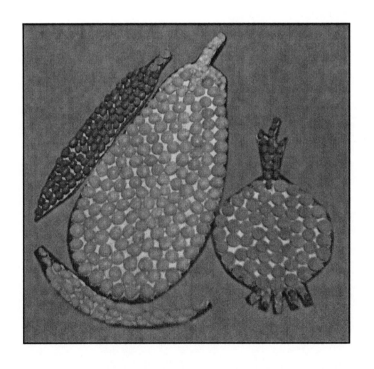

Asha Manoor

To order additional copies of this book, contact:
Xlibris LLC
1-888-795-4274
www.Xlibris.com
Orders@Xlibris.com
143122

Contents

**In memory of my late
mother, who's always
in my heart.**

Dhanyavada (Thanks)

Before I begin to take you on a joyous journey of exploring mouth-watering recipes from the Indian province of Karnataka, I would like to acknowledge my heartfelt thanks to:

my dear mother, who was a great cook and a greater human being. I have never seen such a noble woman in my life. She is the main inspiration behind my venture into writing this cookbook. I can proudly say that I have learned everything about cooking and its intricacies from my ever-giving and selfless mother. Unfortunately, she left all of us to her final abode last year and I am sure that she's blessing me up from the heavens in this endeavour of mine.

my dear father from whom I have imbibed great qualities of life such as, healthy living, honesty and so also planning as well as organization skills.

my dear husband, who's very supportive and also shares my belief in eating healthy, home-made, vegetarian food.

my dear son and my dear daughter, who have always motivated me to prepare as well as serve them with authentic Indian food at home.

my dear son again for his valuable technical inputs in bringing out my passion of cooking alive through this book.

my two sisters and brother with whom I have had memorable times of growing up together in the silicon valley of India, Bengaluru.

my Publishers, Xlibris Book Publishing Company who were instrumental in making my dream of publishing this book come true.

last but not the least, my dear readers without whom I could never dare to think of writing this cookbook even in my wildest dreams!

Introduction

I would like to start the introduction with myself being motivated to be a vegetarian at home by both of my parents, being vegetarians themselves. It's like I was born a vegetarian as my parents never believed in animal killing and instilled the same belief on their children. I have spent most of my growing years in Bengaluru, capital-city of southern province/state of Karnataka. From a very young age, I have observed my mother always cooking fresh, tasty meals and snacks at home for the family. So, eating home-made, fresh meals spiced up with my mother's unconditional love was like a celebration of life on a regular basis for the whole family.

Due to my mother's huge influence on me from a very tender age, cooking became a kind of lifetime passion for me and very soon I realised that it's nothing but a labour of love. So, even when I was studying at University in Bengaluru, sometimes I used to cook evening snacks at home for the whole family (of course with my mother's permission and guidance).

After my marriage and thereafter moving to Delhi, I got exposed to food from northern India too. As such, I am familiar with north Indian as well as south Indian delicacies.

The year-2000 brought us to Canada as immigrants. As we all merged slowly but surely into the Canadian way of living, I used to hear questions from some people like, my children's friends' parents and some neighbours of ours, who were originally from countries other than India, as to how vegetarians could exist only on vegetables! In this connection, I would like to clarify once for all, the misconception that vegetarians eat only vegetables and nothing else.

Vegetarians depend on lentils, beans and peas for their regular intake of proteins. They consume cooked rice or chapatti or roti (flat bread made with wheat flour or rice flour or even millet powder) for their carbohydrates-intake. Vegetables are boiled or cooked or shallow-fried either separately or prepared as curry in combination with lentils or beans or peas. These vegetables or curry are consumed along with rice or roti or chapattis.

As regards to calcium, we include milk and yogurt in our diet. For fat-intake, we use butter, oil or clarified butter (also known as ghee). Fruits are also included in our diet on a regular basis. I hope to have cleared the misconception about vegetarians surviving only on vegetables, to the best of my ability.

Finally, I would like to include a famous quote by the global spiritual leader, Dalai Lama: 'Approach love and cooking with reckless abandon (meaning without inhibitions)'. Not only I believe in the above quote, but also practice in my real life too and trust me, it creates a wonderful feeling at the end of the day to love your family and so also the humanity as a whole. It's a good idea to incorporate this approach in your life too, my dear readers!

Appetizers/Starters

Tomato Rasam

½ cup yellow split peas (arhar dal)
½ tomato (medium-sized)
2 teaspoons rasam powder
¼ teaspoon cur cumin (turmeric)
½ teaspoon mustard seeds
2 teaspoons oil
½ teaspoon tamarind paste
Pinch of asafoetida (hing)
Salt to taste

Cook yellow split peas and tomato with water (2 and ½ cups) in pressure cooker (until five whistles) and allow them to cool. Add rasam powder, tamarind paste, salt as well as 1 ½ cups of water to cooked yellow split peas as well as tomato and boil the mixture on medium heat in a pot to the required consistency (to be little watery like soup).

For seasoning, heat up oil in a pan with mustard seeds, asafoetida (optional) and cur cumin thrown in. When mustard seeds crackle, remove from heat and add it to the boiled mixture above. Stir it well and eat with cooked rice or drink as soup with little butter (optional) added to it.

Onion Pakoda

2 cups chickpea-flour (besan)
4 teaspoons vegetable oil or olive oil or butter
2 medium-sized onions (chopped)
1 cup finely chopped-cilantro (hara dhaniya)
1 cup water
1 teaspoon red chilli powder
Pinch of asafoetida (hing)
Salt to taste
Oil for deep-frying

Mix all the above ingredients in a mixing bowl and make dough out of it. Take small portions of the dough (about the size of small limes), make abstract balls and deep-fry them in oil until they turn golden brown in colour. Cool and serve them as snacks with tea or coffee (pakodas can also be consumed with tomato sauce).

Plantain/Onion/Potato Bonda

2 cups chickpea-flour (besan)
4 teaspoons olive oil/butter
2 plantains/onions/Potatoes (thin slices)
1 teaspoon red chilli powder
1 ½ cups water
Pinch of asafoetida (hing)
Salt to taste
Oil for deep-frying

Mix the above ingredients in a mixing bowl to make dough (a little watery in consistency as compared to onion pakoda). Heat up oil in a deep-frying pan. Dip sliced-vegetables (one by one) in the dough and deep-fry until they turn golden brown in colour. Remove from heat and serve fresh with or without sauce.

Uddina Vade (Vada)

2 cups black gram (urid dal)
2 green chillies (hari mirch)
½ cup chopped cilantro (hara dhaniya)
½ teaspoon whole black pepper (kali mirch)
1 teaspoon chopped ginger (adarakh)
Pinch of asafoetida (hing)
Salt to taste
Oil for deep-frying

Soak black gram overnight (or for at least four to five hours) in water and throw away the water. Grind soaked black gram, green chillies, cilantro, black pepper, ginger, salt and asafoetida (optional) to a fine paste using required amount of water. The paste has to be thick, not watery.

Heat up oil in a deep-frying pan; take small portions of the batter; pat them a little flat using your fingers as well as palm of your hands (you can dip your fingers in water while patting if the batter becomes too sticky to mould) and make small holes (each portion has to have one hole at the centre) and deep-fry in oil until they turn golden brown in colour. Serve Vade/Vada as snacks/part of a meal with chutney/sambar/sauce.

Maddur Vada

4 cups rice flour
1 cup cream wheat lets (rava/sooji)
1 cup all-purpose flour (maida)
5 medium-sized chopped onions
1 teaspoon cumin
3 small green chillies
½ teaspoon red chilli powder
¼ cup chopped curry leaves (optional)
¼ cup chopped cilantro
4 teaspoons butter/ghee
Pinch of asafoetida (hing)
Salt to taste
Oil for deep-frying

Mix all the above ingredients (except for oil) in a bowl and make dough using water. Heat up oil in a deep-frying pan. Make small balls of the dough (the size of a small lime). Make round-patties out of these balls using the palm of your hand as well as fingers and deep-fry until they turn golden brown in colour and serve as snacks with coffee or tea.

Nippattu

3 cups rice flour
1 cup all-purpose flour (maida)
½ cup roasted split chickpeas (chutney dal)
½ cup chopped peanuts
1 teaspoon red chilli powder
3 teaspoons butter/ghee
Pinch of asafoetida (hing)
Salt to taste
Oil for deep-frying

Mix all the above ingredients (except for oil) in a bowl to make dough using water. Heat up oil in a deep-frying pan. Make small balls of the dough (the size of a small lime). Make round-patties out of these balls using the palm of your hand as well as fingers and deep-fry until they turn golden brown in colour and serve as snacks with coffee or tea.

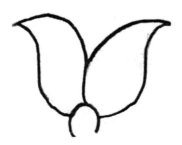

Gojjavalakki (Sour-rice flakes)

2 cups rice flakes (thick-chidwa)
½ cup brown sugar (gud)
1 teaspoon rasam powder
½ teaspoon mustard seeds
¼ teaspoon cur cumin (turmeric)
1 teaspoon tamarind paste
3 teaspoons oil
1 teaspoon dried split chickpeas (chana dal)
2 teaspoons black gram (urid dal)
2 teaspoons white sesame seeds (thil)
12 curry leaves (optional)
½ cup peanuts (moongfali)
Pinch of asafoetida (hing)
Salt to taste

Blend or grind (dry) rice flakes to a coarse texture and soak it in a bowl with tamarind water (can be obtained either by soaking one teaspoon of tamarind in one cup of water; throwing away the pulp after squeezing the juice or by dissolving tamarind paste in one cup of water) and brown sugar, for at least one hour. Then the lumps are to be softened using fingers. Rasam powder and salt are to be added to the soaked rice flakes; mixed well and kept aside.

Heat up oil in a pan; add cur cumin, asafoetida (optional) and mustard seeds. Once mustard seeds crackle, add dried split chickpeas and black gram; allow them to turn golden brown in colour. Add curry leaves to this and allow them to crackle too and remove from heat; add it to the rice flakes-mixture above and mix well again.

Deep-fry half cup of Peanuts (optional) in oil; add it to the mixture above to give a crunchy twist to it and serve as snack with tea or coffee.

Chakkuli

4 cups rice flour
1 cup black gram (urid dal) flour
¼ teaspoon asafoetida (hing)
1 teaspoon red chilli powder
½ cup butter/clarified butter (ghee)
1 teaspoon white sesame seeds
1 teaspoon cumin
Salt to taste
Oil for deep-frying

Mix all the above ingredients (except for oil) thoroughly well in a mixing bowl with water to make big dough. Heat up oil in a deep-frying pan and put chakkuli dough in oil by pressing balls of dough using chakkuli-maker (available in any Indian store and with a plate inside having star-shaped holes). Deep-fry until chakkulis turn golden brown in colour. Remove from heat, cool and serve as snacks with tea or coffee.

Thengolu

4 cups rice flour
2 cups black gram (urid dal) flour
¼ teaspoon asafoetida (hing)
½ cup melted butter/ghee
1 teaspoon white sesame seeds
1 teaspoon cumin
Salt to taste
Oil for deep-frying

Mix the above ingredients (except for oil) thoroughly well in a mixing bowl with water to make big dough. Heat up oil in a deep-frying pan and put thengolu-pieces in oil by pressing balls of dough using chakkuli-maker (available in any Indian store, with a different plate inside having round holes). Deep-fry Thengolu until they turn golden brown in colour. Remove from heat, cool and serve as snacks.

Main course

Rava Idli

3 cups cream wheat lets (rava or sooji)
2 ½ cups yogurt (thick or 3.25%)
½ teaspoon baking powder
2 teaspoons black gram (Urid dal)
2 teaspoons dried split chickpeas (chana dal)
½ teaspoon mustard seeds
¼ teaspoon cur cumin (turmeric)
½ teaspoon baking powder
½ cup finely chopped cilantro (hara dhaniya)
½ cup oil
Pinch of asafoetida (hing)
Salt to taste

Heat up or roast wheat lets in a pan, stirring continuously until they turn light brownish in colour and put them aside. Heat up oil in the pan; add asafoetida, cur cumin and mustard seeds. When mustard seeds crackle, add black gram and dried split chickpeas. Once these turn golden brown in colour, add wheat lets and stir for two minutes; remove from heat thereafter.

Pour the above contents into a mixing bowl and add yogurt, salt as well as baking powder. Mix them thoroughly well so that there are no lumps left behind and keep the mixture closed with a lid for at least thirty minutes. Steam idlis in an Idli-stand (available in any Indian store) or even in an Egg-poacher, cool and serve with chutney or chutney powder or pickle or even sauce.

Masala Dosa

Dosa

4 cups rice (any type except boiled rice)
1 cup black gram (urid dal)
½ cup yellow split peas (arhar dal)
½ cup rice flakes (chidwa)
2 teaspoons fenugreek seeds (methi)
Salt to taste
Oil

Soak the above ingredients (except oil) in water overnight or at least for six to eight hours and grind to a fine paste (neither too thick nor too watery) using required amount of water. Keep this batter aside, covered with a lid, overnight or at least for ten to fourteen hours or until it's fermented well (the level of batter will rise to almost double its depth if fermented well). Once fermented, it is to be refrigerated and can be taken out just before use or otherwise it becomes sour to taste. Salt can be added just before making dosas.

Masala Dosa

Vegetable stuffing
3 medium-sized potatoes
2 medium-sized onions (chopped)
2 green chillies (chopped)
½ teaspoon mustard seeds
1 teaspoon dried split chickpeas (chana dal)
2 teaspoons black gram (urid dal)
¼ teaspoon cur cumin (turmeric)
Pinch of asafoetida (hing)
8-10 curry leaves (optional)
Salt to taste

Boil potatoes, cool and throw off the peel and keep them aside. Heat up oil in a pan; add cur cumin, asafoetida and mustard seeds. When mustard seeds crackle, add curry leaves, black gram, green chillies and dried split chickpeas; allow them to turn golden brown in colour. Add chopped onions to this and cook (with little water at a time) until they become soft. Then, add boiled potatoes and salt, mix thoroughly well and remove from heat.

Masala Dosa

Chutney
½ cup roasted dried split chickpeas (chutney dal)
2 cups fresh coconut (grated)
2 red chillies
1 garlic-bulb
½ cup water
Salt to taste

Mix all the above ingredients and grind to a reasonably fine paste. Heat up a flat pan on medium heat, splash a teaspoon of water onto it and spread dosa batter (about 1½ to 2 big scoops) into a circular-shape of about 6 inch in diameter, by means of a ladle or scoop with rounded bottom. Add half teaspoon of oil on each side of dosa along its circumference. Dosa is to be cooked on both sides by flipping. When dosa turns golden brown in colour, stuff it first with chutney, then with vegetable stuffing (onto the softer side) on half part of dosa. Cover chutney and stuffing with the remaining part of dosa, add half teaspoon butter (optional) and serve hot. Masala Dosa can be consumed for breakfast or lunch or even dinner. It's also served along with sambar in some restaurants.

Ade Dosa

1 cup black gram (urid dal)
1 cup green gram (mung dal)
1 cup dried split chickpeas (chana dal)
1 cup yellow split peas (arhar dal)
1 cup rice
3 medium-sized green chillies
½ cup chopped cilantro (hara dhaniya)
2 teaspoons chopped ginger
6 whole black peppers
Salt to taste

Soak black gram, green gram, dried split chickpeas, yellow split peas and rice in water overnight (or for at least 6-8 hours) Throw away the soaked water and grind them along with green chillies, cilantro, ginger, salt and whole black peppers to a fine paste with fresh water to the required consistency (similar to that of pancake-batter).

Heat up a flat pan on medium heat, splash a teaspoon of water onto it and spread dosa batter (about 1 ½ to 2 big scoops) into a circular shape of about 6 inch in diameter, by means of a ladle or scoop with rounded bottom. Add half teaspoon of oil on each side of dosa along its circumference. Dosa is to be cooked on both sides by flipping. When dosa turns golden brown in colour, fold it into half, add a little butter (optional) and is ready to be served by itself or also with chutney/pickle/sauce.

Ragi Dosa

1 cup black gram (urid dal)
4 cups millet (ragi) flour
6 cups water
1 teaspoon fenugreek seeds (methi)
Salt to taste
Oil

Soak black gram and fenugreek seeds together in water overnight or for at least eight hours. Grind it to a fine paste with one cup of fresh water (throw way the soaked water). Add millet flour, salt, six cups of water; mix it well and keep it closed with a lid overnight or until it rises in level (usually to double its depth) due to fermentation. Once fermented, the batter must be kept in the fridge and to be taken out just before use or otherwise, it will turn sour in taste.

Heat up a flat pan on medium heat, splash a teaspoon of water onto it and spread dosa batter (about 1 ½ to 2 scoops) into a circular shape of about 6 inch in diameter, by means of a ladle or scoop with rounded bottom. Add half teaspoon of oil on each side of dosa along its circumference. Dosa is to be cooked on both sides by flipping. When dosa turns golden brown in colour, fold it into half, add a little butter (optional) and serve with chutney/pickle/sauce.

Rava Dosa

2 cups rice flour
1 cup wheat lets (fine rava/sooji)
1 cup all-purpose flour (maida)
½ teaspoon cumin
2 cups water
Salt to taste
Oil/butter

Mix the above ingredients (except for oil) in a mixing bowl and keep the batter aside closed (with a lid) for at least thirty minutes. Heat up a flat pan, splash one teaspoon of water onto it and spread the batter (about 1 ½ to 2 scoops) into a circular shape of about 6 inch in diameter, with a ladle or scoop with round bottom. Add half teaspoon oil on each side of it (dosa is to be cooked on both sides by flipping) along its circumference. Once dosa turns crispy and golden brown in colour, fold it into half; add a little butter onto it (optional) and serve hot with chutney/pickle/sauce.

Onion Rice

3 cups rice (cooked)
1 medium-sized onion (chopped)
½ teaspoon mustard seeds
2 green chillies (chopped)
½ teaspoon black gram (urid dal)
½ teaspoon dried split chickpeas (chana dal)
Lime juice (1/2 portion of lime)
Salt to taste
¼ teaspoon cur cumin (turmeric)
3 teaspoons oil
3 teaspoons peanuts (optional)
Pinch of asafoetida (hing)
Oil to deep-fry peanuts

Heat up oil in a pan and add mustard seeds, cur cumin (turmeric) and asafoetida. When mustard seeds crackle, add black gram, dried split chickpeas, green chillies and stir well. When black gram and dried split chickpeas turn golden brown in colour, add chopped onion as well as salt, stir for two minutes and then add water in small quantities at a time until it's cooked and soft. Remove from heat and keep it aside. Deep-fry peanuts in a pan. Cook rice and mix three cups of it thoroughly well with cooked onion, squeezed lime juice and deep-fried peanuts (optional) in a mixing bowl and serve.

Note: Although generally one cup of rice needs two and a half cups of water to cook, some varieties may require more.

Rava Uppittu (Upma)

2 cups wheat lets (rava or sooji)
3 cups water
1 big onion (chopped)
1 ½ teaspoon black gram (urid dal)
1 teaspoon dried split chickpeas (chana dal)
¼ teaspoon cur cumin (turmeric)
12 curry leaves (optional)
½ teaspoon mustard seeds
3 small green chillies
4 teaspoons oil
Lime juice (1/2 portion of lime)
Pinch of asafoetida (hing)
Salt to taste

Roast/heat up wheat lets in a pan, by continuously stirring until they turn light brownish in colour and put them aside. Heat up oil in the pan; add asafoetida, cur cumin and mustard seeds. When mustard seeds crackle, add black gram and dried split chickpeas. Once these turn golden brown in colour, add curry leaves, green chillies and onion and stir well for two minutes. Cook this by using small amount of water at a time until onion-pieces are soft; add wheat lets and mix well. Add three cups of water, salt to it and let it cook until wheat lets are soft. Remove it from heat, add lime juice, mix it well and serve hot as breakfast or snack.

Vegetable fried rice

3 cups rice (cooked)
2 cups of any vegetable (cut into about size: 1 inch length &
½ inch width; single vegetable or a combination of vegetables
such as eggplant, carrot, peas, bell peppers or capsicum)
½ teaspoon mustard seeds
1 ½ teaspoon sambar powder
½ teaspoon black gram (urid dal)
½ teaspoon dried split chickpeas (chana dal)
Salt to taste
¼ teaspoon cur cumin (turmeric)
3 teaspoons oil
¼ cup grated coconut
Pinch of asafoetida (hing)

Cook three cups of rice and keep it aside. Heat up oil in a pan; add mustard seeds, cur cumin (turmeric) and asafoetida. When mustard seeds crackle, add black gram, dried split chickpeas and stir well. Once black gram and dried split chickpeas turn golden brown in colour, add vegetables as well as salt, stir for about five minutes and then add water in small quantities at a time until they are cooked and soft. Once vegetables are cooked, add sambar powder and grated coconut; continue to stir for about five to ten minutes so that the vegetables absorb spice well and remove from heat. Mix these spiced vegetables with cooked rice thoroughly and serve.

Ragi Mudde /Balls

1 cup millet (ragi) flour
2 cups water
½ teaspoon oil
¼ cup cooked rice
Salt to taste

Boil water with oil and salt. Add ragi flour and cooked rice to this and allow it to cook, stirring continuously until all lumps are softened. Once cooked well, remove from heat; make balls (lime-sized) and serve with sambar/rasam/curry for lunch or dinner.

Bisibele bhath

2 cups yellow split peas
1 cup rice
1 cup chopped spinach
½ cup chopped onions
½ cup peeled and chopped potatoes
½ cup green peas
½ cup chopped cabbage
½ cup chopped carrots
½ cup chopped beans
3 teaspoons sambar powder
3 teaspoons oil
½ teaspoon mustard seeds
¼ teaspoon cur cumin (turmeric)
1 teaspoon tamarind paste
Salt to taste
Pinch of asafoetida (hing)

Half-cook yellow split peas with four cups of water in pressure cooker (two whistles) or in a pot; add rice and more water (two cups). Continue to cook in the pot until rice is 75% cooked; add vegetables and cook until they are soft. When yellow split peas, rice and vegetables are all cooked well, add sambar powder, salt, tamarind paste and two more cups of water and mix it well. Boil the mixture until the required consistency is met with (not watery) and remove from heat.

For seasoning, heat up oil in a pan; add cur cumin, asafoetida (optional) and mustard seeds. Once mustard seeds crackle, remove from heat and add it to the above mixture, serve hot for lunch or dinner.

Vegetable Pulav

3 cups rice (cooked)
½ cup green beans (cut into 1 inch pieces)
½ cup carrots (cut into 1 inch pieces)
¼ cup roasted chickpeas (chutney dal)
½ cup chopped onions
½ cup green peas
¼ teaspoon cur cumin (turmeric)
5 fresh mint leaves
3 small cinnamon sticks
3 small green chillies
3 cloves
¼ cup chopped cilantro
½ teaspoon cumin
3 teaspoons oil
½ teaspoon mustard seeds
½ cup grated coconut
Pinch of asafoetida
Salt to taste

Boil or steam green beans, carrots, green peas and onions together and keep aside. Cook three cups of rice and keep it aside. Grind cinnamon sticks, roasted split chickpeas, mint leaves, grated coconut, green chillies, cilantro, asafoetida, cumin together with water to make a reasonably fine paste of spices. Heat up oil in a pot; add cur cumin, asafoetida and mustard seeds. Once mustard seeds crackle, add boiled vegetables as well as the spice-paste and mix well. Add half cup more water and salt to it, mix again and boil the mixture until it's no longer watery. Mix this with cooked rice and serve fresh for either lunch or dinner.

Chapatti

2 cups wheat flour (aata)
2 teaspoons oil
Salt to taste

Mix the above ingredients in a mixing bowl and make big dough out of this mixture, using water. The dough has to be very smooth (by kneading it very well) to make soft chapattis. Keep the dough closed with a lid for about thirty minutes. Heat up a flat pan (on medium heat). Roll chapattis of about 6 inch-diametric circular shape, using a rolling pin on a rolling board, taking small portions of dough, the size of lime. Chapattis have to be rolled neither too thick nor too thin or otherwise they will not be light and fluffy. Cook chapattis (both sides have to be cooked by flipping) either with oil (half teaspoon on each side) or without and serve hot with chutney/ curry/potato stuffing/pickle.

Poori

2 cups wheat flour
2 teaspoons oil
Salt to taste
Oil for deep-frying

Mix wheat flour, oil and salt in a mixing bowl to make big dough, using water. The dough is to be kneaded thoroughly well to make good, fluffy pooris. Heat up oil in a deep-frying pan (on medium heat). Roll pooris into circular shape of 4 inch diameter using small portions of dough, half the size of a lime. Deep-fry these in oil until they turn golden brown in colour (pooris have to be deep-fried on both sides by flipping); cool and serve with saagu or potato stuffing or even chutney.

Vegetable stews/Side dishes

Sambar/Curry

1 cup yellow split peas (arhar dal)
3 cups mixed vegetables (cut into about one inch-sized pieces)
½ tomato (medium-sized)
3 teaspoons sambar powder
Pinch of asafoetida (hing)
¼ teaspoon cur cumin (turmeric)
½ teaspoon mustard seeds
3 teaspoons oil
1 teaspoon tamarind paste
10 curry leaves (optional)
Salt to taste

Cook yellow split peas and tomato with three cups of water in Pressure cooker (until five whistles) and let it cool. Steam or boil vegetables. Mix cooked yellow split peas, tomato, steamed/boiled vegetables and tamarind paste in a pot. Add two more cups of water, salt, curry leaves, sambar powder to it and boil until the required consistency is met with and remove from heat.

For seasoning, heat up oil in a pan; add mustard seeds, asafoetida (optional) and cur cumin. Once mustard seeds crackle, remove from heat and add it to the boiled mixture above. Stir it well and sambar is ready to be consumed with rice or chapatti/roti as a meal for either lunch or dinner.

Dal

½ cup yellow split peas (arhar dal)
½ cup of any lentil/combination of lentils
4 cups of water
3 medium-sized potatoes
2 green chillies (chopped or sliced vertically along the length)
½ cup cilantro (chopped)
¼ teaspoon cur cumin (turmeric)
1 teaspoon cumin
1 teaspoon ginger (chopped)
1 teaspoon garlic (chopped)
Pinch of asafoetida (hing)
Salt to taste
Squeezed lime juice (1/2 portion)
3 teaspoons oil

Cook yellow split peas and lentils together with four cups of water in pressure cooker (4 whistles). Boil potatoes in water, throw the peel away; break them into pieces and keep them aside. Heat up oil in pot/pan; add cur cumin, asafoetida and cumin. Once cumin turns brown in colour, add ginger, garlic and green chillies. When garlic and ginger become brown in colour, add cooked lentils and yellow split peas, green chillies, salt and two more cups of water. Boil the whole mixture until its consistency becomes like that of tomato ketchup. Remove from heat; add cilantro and lime juice; mix well and serve with rice or roti for lunch or dinner.

Potato stuffing for Roti-roll/Bread-sandwich

3 medium-sized potatoes
3 teaspoons oil
1 teaspoon black gram (urid dal)
1 teaspoon dried split chickpeas (chana dal)
½ teaspoon mustard seeds
2 green chillies
¼ teaspoon cur cumin (turmeric)
¼ cup cilantro (chopped)
Pinch of asafoetida (hing)

Boil potatoes in water, throw the peel away; break them into pieces and keep them aside. Heat up oil in a pan; add cur cumin, asafoetida and mustard seeds. Allow the seeds to crackle and then add dried split chickpeas, black gram and green chillies. Once black gram and dried split chickpeas turn golden brown in colour, add boiled potatoes, salt and cilantro, and mix them well. Remove from heat, stuff the required quantity inside a rolled roti or between two toasted bread slices (as sandwich) and serve.

Vegetable palya

*3 cups cut (small) vegetable such as
Cabbage/Beans/Carrots/Spinach
2 small green chillies
½ teaspoon mustard seeds
½ cup grated coconut
¼ teaspoon cur cumin (turmeric)
1 teaspoon black gram (urid dal)
1 teaspoon dried split chickpeas (chana dal)
Pinch of asafoetida (hing)
3 teaspoons oil
Salt to taste*

Steam or boil vegetables and keep them aside. Heat up oil in a pan; add cur cumin, asafoetida (optional) and mustard seeds. Once mustard seeds crackle, add green chilies, black gram and dried split chickpeas. When black gram and dried split chickpeas turn golden brown in colour, add steamed vegetables, coconut and salt; mix well for two minutes; remove from heat and serve hot with roti/chapatti/rice or even with bread toast.

Spicy Vegetable palya

3 cups cut (small) vegetable such as
Cabbage/Beans/Carrots/Spinach
1 teaspoon sambar powder
½ teaspoon mustard seeds
½ cup grated coconut
¼ teaspoon cur cumin (turmeric)
1 teaspoon black gram (urid dal)
1 teaspoon dried split chickpeas (chana dal)
Pinch of asafoetida (hing)
3 teaspoons oil
Salt to taste

Steam or boil vegetables and keep them aside. Heat up oil in a pan; add cur cumin, asafoetida (optional) and mustard seeds. Once mustard seeds crackle, add black gram and dried split chickpeas. When black gram and dried split chickpeas turn golden brown in colour, add steamed vegetables, sambar powder, coconut and salt; mix well and continue stirring for five minutes; remove from heat and serve hot with roti/chapatti/rice or even bread toast.

Saagu for Roti/Poori

1 cup chopped spinach
1 cup chopped cabbage
1 cup chopped green beans
½ cup carrots (cut into small pieces)
½ cup chopped onions
½ cup peeled & chopped potatoes
½ cup grated coconut
5 small cinnamon sticks
5 cloves
3 small green chillies
¼ cup chopped cilantro
8 fresh mint leaves (optional)
½ teaspoon cumin
3 teaspoons oil
½ teaspoon mustard seeds
Salt to taste
Pinch of asafoetida (hing)
½ cup roasted split chickpeas (chutney dal)
¼ teaspoon cur cumin (turmeric)

Boil or steam all vegetables and keep them aside. Grind cinnamon sticks, roasted split chickpeas, cloves, grated coconut, green chillies, cilantro, mint-leaves, and cumin together to a reasonably fine paste by using water. Mix this paste with boiled vegetables; add salt and two more cups of water and mix well. Boil this mixture in a pot on medium heat until the required consistency (not watery) is met with.

Heat up oil in a pan; add cur cumin, asafoetida (optional) and mustard seeds. Allow mustard seeds to crackle and add it to the boiled mixture. Saagu is ready to be served with roti or poori or even with cooked-rice.

Majjige Huli (Buttermilk-sambar)

6 teaspoons dried split chickpeas (chana dal)
4 teaspoons yellow split peas (arhar dal)
½ cup grated coconut
3 small green chillies
1 teaspoon cumin
½ cup chopped cilantro
Cut vegetables (medium cubes) such as Squash/cucumber/
okra/green pepper or combination of them
½ *teaspoon mustard seeds*
3 teaspoons oil
¼ *teaspoon cur cumin (turmeric)*
1 cup yogurt
Pinch of asafoetida (hing)
Salt to taste

Soak dried split chickpeas and yellow split peas together in water for at least one hour. Grind these two soaked-ingredients with grated coconut, green chillies, cumin, asafoetida (optional) and cilantro to reasonably fine spice-paste using water and keep it aside. Steam or boil cucumber/squash/green pepper (okra has to be cooked with oil to avoid stickiness). Mix boiled vegetables, the spice-paste, salt as well as yogurt in a pot; add three more cups of water. Bring this mixture to a boil (or to the required consistency).

For seasoning, heat up oil in a pan; add cur cumin, asafoetida (optional) and mustard seeds. Once mustard seeds crackle, remove from heat and add it to the boiled mixture; mix well and serve hot with cooked rice for lunch or dinner.

Desserts/Sweetmeats

Mysore Pak

1 cup chickpea-flour
2 ½ cups sugar
2 cups butter or ghee (clarified butter)
½ teaspoon baking powder
½ cup water

Heat up chickpea-flour in a pan for five minutes, stirring continuously to soften any lumps and keep it aside. Mix sugar and water in a deep-frying pan on medium heat and allow sugar to melt. Add butter or ghee to it; when it melts and mixes well with sugary water, add heated chickpea-flour to it; keep stirring the mixture continuously until it becomes thick, and doesn't stick to the pan anymore. Add baking powder to this and mix it well again for two minutes. To test if done, remove a small portion (teaspoonful) of this mixture, put it in a small bowl of water to see if it comes out as a single piece with the texture of fudge, without dissolving in water. Pour the mixture onto a plate, smeared with a little butter or ghee, cool, cut into diamond or square-shaped pieces; serve as dessert.

Besan Ladoo

2 cups chickpea-flour
1 ½ cups grounded sugar
¼ cup raisins
¼ cup cashews
½ cup butter/ghee
½ teaspoon cardamom powder

Heat up butter/ghee in a pan; add chickpea-flour and continue stirring until it turns light brown in colour, giving a roasted smell and remove from heat. Deep-fry cashews and raisins separately. Mix these fried dry fruits thoroughly well with heated chickpea-flour, sugar and cardamom powder. Make small balls (ladoos) out of this mixture using palm and fingers of your hands. If it's hard to make balls, add a small quantity of milk and ladoos are ready for dessert.

Coconut Barfi

2 cups grated coconut
2 cups sugar
2 cups milk
¼ teaspoon cardamom powder/rose-essence
¼ teaspoon baking powder

Mix the above ingredients (except for baking powder) in a pan/pot and put it on medium heat. Continue to stir until coconut becomes soft, cooked and the mixture turns thick. To test if done, remove a small portion (a teaspoonful) of the mixture; put in a small bowl of water and check by hand if it comes out as a single piece. Add baking powder to it; stir again for one minute and pour the mixture onto a plate (smeared with a little butter); cool and cut into diamond-shaped pieces and serve as dessert.

Puri Ladoo

100 grams puffed rice (puri/murmura)
100 grams brown sugar (jaggery)
4 teaspoons water
2 teaspoons butter/ Clarified butter (ghee)

Heat up brown sugar, water and butter together in a pan. Stir the mixture continuously until it becomes thick in consistency. To test if done, add a small portion of it into a small bowl of water to see if it hardens immediately and comes out as a single piece. Remove the mixture from heat. Add puffed rice to this thick syrup; mix well and make small balls (ladoos) out of this using palm and fingers of your hands; serve as dessert.

Rava/Sooji Ladoo

2 cups cream wheat lets (fine rava/sooji)
1 ½ cups grounded sugar
½ cup butter/clarified butter (ghee)
¼ cup raisins
¼ cup cashews
¼ teaspoon cardamom powder

Heat up butter in a pan and add wheat lets; roast until they turn light golden brown in colour. Deep-fry raisins and cashews separately in butter or oil and mix with roasted wheat lets, sugar and cardamom powder in a mixing bowl. Make small balls (ladoos-the size of a small lime) using the palm as well as fingers of your hands and serve as dessert. If it's difficult to make balls, add a little milk at a time and try making them.

Vermicelli Payasa (Pudding)

2 cups vermicelli
2 cups milk (thick or 3.25%)
1 cup sugar
2 teaspoons butter or ghee
¼ teaspoon cardamom powder
3 teaspoons cashews (optional)
3 teaspoons raisins (optional)

Heat up butter in a pan; add vermicelli and roast it until it turns golden brown in colour; add milk and continue to stir until vermicelli is cooked and soft. Add sugar; stir for five minutes or until sugar melts and mixes well with vermicelli as well as milk. Deep-fry cashews and raisins separately, mix them with the above mixture and payasa (pudding) is ready to be served as dessert. It can also be refrigerated to enjoy a cold pudding. If pudding is too thick, a little more milk can be added to it.

Glossary

1 cup-measure: 250 milliliters
1 teaspoon-measure: 5 milliliters
1 tablespoon-measure: 15 milliliters
Aata/Hittu: Dough
Achar/Uppinakayi: Pickle
Adarakh/Shunti: Ginger
Ade: Mixture of beans and peas
Aloo/Aloogedde: Potatoes
Arhar dal/Thogari bele: Yellow split peas
Bada Chamach/Dodda soutu: Ladle/scoop
Barfi/Mithai: Fudge
Besan/Kadale hittu: Chickpea-flour
Bhindi/Bendekayi: Okra
Bonda/Pakoda: Fried nuggets
Chakkuli: Deep-fried, spiced, rice-rounds/pieces
Chamach/Chamacha: Spoon
Chana dal/Kadale bele: Dried split chickpeas
Chawal/Akki: Rice
Chidwa/Avalakki: Rice flakes
Chini/Sakkare: Sugar

Dahi/Mosaru: Yogurt
Dal/Bele: Lentils/Peas
Dalchini: Cinnamon
Elakki/Elaichi: Cardamom
Gehoon/Godhi: Wheat
Ghee/Thuppa: Clarified butter, prepared by boiling butter
Groundnuts/Kadalekayi: Peanuts
Gud/Bella: Jaggery
Hara dhaniya/Kottambari soppu: Cilantro
Hari mirch/Hasi menasinakayi: Green chillies
Hing/Ingu: Asafoetida
Hurigadale/Chutney dal: Roasted dried split chickpeas
Idli: Rice dumpling
Imli/Hunisehannu: Tamarind
Jaggery/Bella: Brown sugar
Jeera/Jeerige: Cumin
Kadi patta/Karibevu: Curry leaves
Kheer/Payasa: Pudding
Ladoo: Ball
Lahasun/Bellulli: Garlic
Lal mirch/Kempu menasinakayi: Red chillies
Lal Mirch powder/Ona kharada pudi: Red chilli powder
Lassi/Majjige: Butter milk
Laung/Lavanga: Clove
Masala/Masale: Spice
Matar/Bataani: Green peas
Maida/Maida hittu: All purpose-flour
Methi/Menthya: Fenugreek
Moongfali/Kadalekayi: Peanuts/Groundnuts
Mudde: Ball
Mung dal/Hesaru bele: Green gram
Namak/Uppu: Salt
Nariyal/Kobbari: Coconut
Palak/Soppu: Spinach

Pooris: Deep-fried, Fluffy rotis
Pudina: Mint leaves
Puri/Murmura: Puffed rice
Pyaz/Yirulli: Onions
Ragi: Millet
Rava/Sooji: Wheat lets
Rayi/Sasive: Mustard seeds
Ricotta cheese: Cottage cheese
Roti/Chapatti: Indian flat bread
Saagu: Spiced mixture of steamed/boiled vegetables
Sabzi/Tharakari: Vegetable
Sambar/Huli: Curry
Tadka/Vaggarane: Seasoning
Thengolu: Deep-fried rice-rounds/pieces
Thil/Yellu: Sesame seeds
Turmeric/Arishina: Cur cumin
Urid dal/Uddina bele: Black gram
Vada/Vade: Deep-fried black gram nuggets

Note: I have tried my best to translate most of the important words used in above recipes into two Indian languages, Hindi (Indian national language) and Kannada (my mother tongue as well as the language spoken in South Indian province of Karnataka), in that order.

CPSIA information can be obtained at www.ICGtesting.com
Printed in the USA
LVOW12s0006260814

400824LV00002B/404/P

9 781493 124824